for Katharine

First published 1983 by Editions Gallimard
First published 1984 in Great Britain
by Moonlight Publishing Ltd,
36 Stratford Road, London W8
© 1983 by Editions Gallimard
English text © 1984 by Moonlight Publishing Ltd

Printed in Italy by La Editoriale Libraria
ISBN 1 85103 097 2

PAINTING AND PAINTERS

DISCOVERERS

by Adrian Sington
Illustrations by Tony Ross

MOONLIGHT PUBLISHING

Hello, my name is Gilles

After **Watteau,** *Gilles*.

I am a cheerful fellow. I love clowning around and making people laugh at carnivals and circuses. But I'm not just a clown. Come with me and I'll show you.

I was created in 1717 by the sensitive paintbrush of my master, Antoine Watteau. Since then thousands of visitors have admired me in the Louvre in Paris. But the illustrator has helped me escape, so that together we can show you the world I come from, the world of painting and painters.

The illustrator has enjoyed exploring my world too. Ever since images were first created, they have been copied both as a mark of respect and to improve technique. All great painters have copied pictures. That is why Tony Ross has done his own versions of pictures rather than always using reproductions. You'll find both reproductions* of great paintings, and pictures 'in the manner of great artists in the pages that follow.

*marked by a ●

Painters through the ages

First Painters

Og, the Stone Age man (1) was a very important member of his tribe because it was thought he had the power to 'capture' the animals he painted on the walls of the caves they lived in. They thought that this made it easier to hunt them.

Etela, the Etruscan (2) was in charge of painting tombs with pictures of musicians, friends, food and drink so that they could enjoy themselves together when they all came to life in the next world.

Poor Epidaurus, the Greek (3) painted religious pictures. But the government banned them and smashed all the images they could find. So Epidaurus had to paint in secret.

The first famous painters

Jan van Eyck (4) was the first painter to become really famous. Painters like him and Michelangelo (5) were so brilliant that everybody

1. **Og.** Inhabitant of the caves at Lascaux, France – 15,000 BC.

2. **Etela,** Etruscan 500 BC.

3. **Epidaurus,** Greek AD 800.

4. **Van Eyck,** Flemish (1390?-1441)

admired them, including kings and popes of the time. They died rich and famous.

Not so Rembrandt (6). His early career was very successful but gradually he started to paint darker and darker pictures. Nobody wanted them and he died penniless. Today, of course, everybody thinks they are wonderful.

Géricault (7) died very young, only 33 years old. He was the first Romantic painter and painted huge tragic canvasses.

Monet (8) is at the top. Though he was a heavy drinker he was one of the great masters of 19th century painting and turned the public's artistic tastes upside down.

And today's painter (9)...

(Underneath the name of each painter are his dates. To get an idea of the time in which he lived, turn to the time chart on pages 88-89.)

5. **Michelangelo,** Italian (1475-1564)

6. **Rembrandt,** Dutch (1606-1669)

7. **Géricault,** French (1791-1824)

8. **Monet,** French (1840-1926)

Cave art

1. Green and brown paint 'pots' and a stopper.

2. Brushes of moss, leaves and animal hair.

Using bones to crush the earth.

One day in 1940, two children were walking with their dog through the hills around Lascaux in the Dordogne, France. Suddenly the dog disappeared. The children searched for ages and eventually found him deep inside a cave. And what a cave! The walls were covered in buffaloes, bulls, horses and antelopes. Here you can see a horse, wounded by hunters' spears. The stags are pictured holding their heads up in this strange way to show that they are swimming. They have been there for over 15,000 years.

Making Stone Age paints

Just as all artists had to, until the arrival of paint shops in the 18th century, Stone Age painters mixed their own paints. They used things like crushed earth mixed with blood, fat or plant juice to make red, brown and yellow paints. They stored them in hollow bones with lumps of fat for stoppers. The paint was applied with bits of moss or brushes made with animal hair or leaves tied to bone or stick (our paint-brushes today are still hair on a stick). Because the walls to be painted were deep inside the cave some light was needed. Burning moss dipped in animal fat did the trick.

The tale of the foot

1. *Tomb of Memma*, 2000 BC (Thebes, Egypt).

2. *Woman carrying offering*, 1500 BC (Tiryns, Crete).

You can understand a lot about how early painting changed by studying how feet were painted.

Egypt and Crete

Two thousand years ago, Egyptian artists painted figures with two left feet (1). From the side you see two big toes. Five hundred years later, Cretan painters discovered the little toe (2). If you look at the woman carrying the vase she has a right foot.

Greeks and Romans

But on the large Greek vase (3) decorated 1000 years later, for the first time the foot is seen from the front, the soldier's foot. It looks real, so real that the soldier has jumped down from the vase to go and admire the Roman's foot (4) painted 400 years later.

Convention

Egyptian painters were not only trying to imitate life, they were mak-

ing magic, making a world to last past death. It was more important for the people they painted to be right than to look real, so they worked out a way, a convention, to make sure that all went well. Painters all copied this convention. The feet, heads, arms and legs were painted from the side, but the single eye and shoulders were painted from the front. Furthermore the men were always painted taller and darker than the women.

Where does our art come from?

Egyptian art influenced Greek art which in turn was used as a model by the Romans, so it could be said that the Egyptians started Western art.

4. **Roman,** 100 BC (Pompeii).

3. **The Warrior's Leavetaking,** 500 BC (Greece).

Illumination

Barbarians destroyed Rome in AD 455, and painting and the new religion of Christianity found themselves under attack. The Christians had to paint their religious images in secret.

Gradually things eased up, and painters crept out into the open. First they still painted small pictures which could be easily hidden. Then finally they were free to paint as they wished, and painted pictures in enormous bibles or prayer books on parchment.

We are in a nunnery. Most of this type of illustration or illumination was done by monks or nuns. It is called 'illumination' because the pictures 'light up' the page. The nuns by the window write the words – a part of the bible or a prayer – and do the very difficult painting. In the middle two nuns are mixing paints. On the end of the table you can see a pile of pages made from clean vellum. The nun on the right is sewing together the finished pages to make a book. I am looking after the gold leaf, which is very thin indeed, it is also very expensive but it is wonderful for decorating books.

Out of one sheepskin one can make 16 pages of what is called *vellum*. Though it can be made from goat or pig, the finest vellum is made from calf and sheepskin.

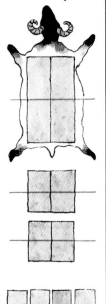

A nugget of gold the size of a golf ball will flatten out if you hammer it into a sheet of gold leaf the size of a football pitch.

Frescoes

In Italian, *fresco* means 'fresh', because the plaster surface on to which the artist paints, must be fresh or wet. First the picture or 'cartoon' is drawn on paper. The paper is attached to the wall and pinholes are made round the drawing. Coal dust shaken onto the paper goes through

Frescoes were used in churches to tell stories of the bible and saints to people who could not read.

After **Giotto,** Italian (1267-1337): *St Francis preaching to the birds.*

Giotto is supervising the painting of the fresco. Assistants painted the background and landscapes. The master painted the heads and anything of interest. Giotto had such a sure touch that he never used a cartoon: he painted directly on to the plaster.

1. Bag of coaldust.
2. Board for spreading plaster on the wall.
3. Paint brush made from animal hair, usually pig.

the holes on to the wall. The painting must be done fast, working downwards so that drips won't damage the finished parts. If the plaster dries before the end of the work, the paint will flake off later. If the painting is completed in time, it will be preserved for centuries.

17

Becoming a painter

After **Paolo Uccello,** Italian (1396-1479): *The Rout of San Romano.*

Piero Medici, illustrious patron and ruler of Florence is well pleased with Uccello's new masterpiece. Here he is giving Uccello some extra money. Uccello has been forced to take on a young nobleman from Milan to please Piero Medici. He cannot paint at all. Look at the mess he is making of my portrait.

In the 14th century groups of painters got together and formed clubs or 'guilds'. The guilds fixed the amount artists got paid and helped arrange work. This meant that by the 15th century most master painters could afford to have studios with apprentices and assistants.

Uccello's studio

The master of this studio is Paolo Uccello. Uccello painted huge panels like this one of the Battle of San Romano. He was interested in conveying movement and experimenting with perspective, one of the first painters to do so. Here the knights' lances stick up in all directions while the cavaliers attack each other.

Paolo Uccello means 'Paul the Bird' in Italian. It is thought he was called this because as an apprentice to Ghiberti, a great Florentine artist, he painted some exceptionally beautiful pictures of birds.

A picture this huge (3.2m x 1.8m) could only have been painted with the help of his apprentices and assistants. Here you can see three *assistants* working on another painting. It is known as a *triptych* because it has three sections. Assistants are allowed to do underdrawing, paint in backgrounds and lay the gold leaf down. The *apprentices* prepare the panels, make brushes and mix paints. They must also learn Bible stories and practise drawing.

Studios were usually on the ground floor of the artist's house, with large doors facing the street so that buyers could come and go.

19

Oil painting

Jan van Eyck,
Flemish (1390?-
1441).

The Betrothal of the Arnolfini ●
(National Gallery, London).

Detail of the mirror

In Belgium, pictures were painted on wood. They couldn't paint frescoes, because Belgium has a damp climate and frescoes could go mouldy. Italian painters used wood too, but they used a paint called *tempera*. Tempera was made from paint powder, water and egg yolk, and it dried very quickly. In Belgium, Jan van Eyck and his brother Hubert invented a new type of paint that was to revolutionize painting technique. They mixed paint powder with oil instead of water. *Oil-paint* dries very slowly, so that Jan could work in a lot more detail. Everyone who saw Jan's pictures said that you could smell the flowers Jan painted, they looked so real.

The picture on the left, *The Betrothal of the Arnolfini* has been signed 'Johannes de Eyck fuit hic 1434' (Jan van Eyck was here, 1434). Jan was commissioned by a rich Italian banker living in Flanders to capture the moment of his betrothal. For the couple this picture is practically a marriage contract. If you look at the mirror you can see that in the doorway there are even two witnesses to the marriage. One man in blue (who is probably Jan himself) and another in red.

Jan used oak panels for his pictures. The oak tree was cut into rounds (above), of which only the middle part is suitable; the spring of the wood grain causes the outer bits to warp. These middle strips are then joined together and coated with a white base ready for use.

The sign above the door shows a carpenter's shop. This is where painters bought their panels. In the early days carpenters sometimes sold them poor-quality panels, which split after painting, until the government passed a law that all wood panels had to be tested before use.

Hieronymous Bosch Flemish (1450?-1516)

At the end of the Middle Ages in a Belgian town rich and famous for its cloth industry, organ building and bell making lived a painter called

Hieronymous Bosch. Now it was not only the Church and aristocracy that could afford to buy paintings but rich merchants too, and they did not only want religious pictures. Bosch accommodated their desires up to a point. He didn't paint their portraits as van Eyck had before him but let his imagination run riot in depictions of hell and paradise. His imagination was very rich and his pictures are full of demons – half-man, half-animal – cruelly tormenting mortal men. Inevitably, he ran into trouble with the Church authorities over some of his pictures. His paintings are allegories – he uses characters and objects as symbols to represent an idea. In this picture of *The Haywain*, the people grabbing at hay show that there is no point in being greedy because you end up with something of no value – like the hay.

'Hell': panel from *The Haywain* (Prado, Madrid)

The Haywain (central panel) ●: The monsters are pulling the cart to hell. You can see a pope, some musicians, and a demon on the top painted blue because in those days the colour blue symbolized trickery. At the top of the picture Jesus is judging who should go to heaven and who to hell.

Engraving

During the 15th century printing was developed. Pictures were printed using engraved wood blocks. At last those endless journeys carrying huge pictures across Europe were at an end. Now, the painting could be drawn by an engraver and printed on a small piece of paper. Pictures became much more widely available.

Relief engraving (1)
To make a woodcut the artist traces his design in the wood and makes it stand out by scooping out all the bits of wood that are not part of the picture. Then he coats the surface with ink and presses the woodblock onto a piece of paper. The drawing which is in relief appears black on the paper.

Intaglio engraving (2)
The scene on the right has been inspired by a copper engraving by the German artist Albrecht Dürer. For copper engraving another method – intaglio – is used. The artist gouges out his design on a copper block, puts ink in the grooves, wipes the top surface clean and presses damp paper into the grooves using a heavy weight. The grooves print on the paper.

After **Albrecht Dürer,** German (1471-1528): *Saint Eustace.*

Eustace, out hunting, saw a stag with a cross between its antlers and was immediately converted to Christianity. The rider is waiting to carry news of this amazing story, as depicted in Dürer's engraving, from Germany to Italy.

The Renaissance

At the beginning of the 15th century in Italy, artists started to throw off the ideas of the Middle Ages and rediscover the ideals of Ancient Greece and Rome. This universal transformation has come to be called 'The Renaissance' which means rebirth. The age of anonymity was over, artists were hungry for fame.

Artists were eager for knowledge. They wanted to understand how things worked so as to paint them better. All branches of knowledge were fired by this new enthusiasm, writers and philosophers, physicians, architects, sculptors and painters, and from all over Europe, not just Italy.

Here standing on the pinnacle are the champions of the Renaissance.
1. **Dante**, poet (1265-1321).
2. **Brunelleschi**, architect who designed the dome on which they stand (1377-1447).
3. **Lorenzo the Magnificent**, ruler of Florence, patron of the Arts (1449-1492).
4. **Michelangelo**, sculptor, painter, architect (1475-1564).
5. . . . Gilles.

Drawing

Turn to page 40 and try to draw the man on the horse. Does it look like him or not? Now get some tracing paper with a grid of squares drawn on to it and place it on top of the man on the horse. From this, copy what you see in each box onto a clean sheet of paper. It's much easier, isn't it? This procedure was often used by painters, like the one on the right. It helped them to get the angles and proportions of the model right.

Studio drawing: the model

Some of the first people to use drawing were monks. When decorating their manuscripts, the monks drew an outline before filling it in with paint. But there were other reasons for drawing too. Renaissance artists were constantly looking for ways to improve their already impressive technique. One of the best ways was to pay models to pose for hours on end while the artists painted them in different positions and from all angles in crayon, in pastel or in charcoal. This helped them to see how a body worked.

Open air sketching: the country-side

In the Renaissance painters also started to go out of their studios to

Pencil

Pastel

make sketches of the countryside from which they would paint a full-sized landscape.

I am sure you recognize the two people at the bottom of the page. Before starting to paint, Jan van Eyck (p.20) often drew a rough outline annotated with numbers which represented the colours he intended to use.

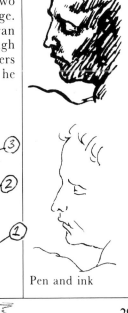

Pen and ink

Leonardo da Vinci
Italian (1452-1519)

Mona Lisa ●(Louvre, Paris).

The Proportions of Man ●

What is the most famous painting in the world? The *Mona Lisa*, of course. Who painted it? Leonardo da Vinci, of course. This masterpiece still astonishes the experts. They have examined the picture under a microscope but there is no trace of the marks made by the paint brush. Is it magic? Almost. For Leonardo was an astonishing man!

He first started painting in the studio of a painter called Verrocchio. One day Verrocchio came down from breakfast and saw Leonardo finishing the left hand angel in his picture of the *Baptism of Jesus*. It was so good that Verrocchio threw away his paint brushes and never painted again. The picture remains unfinished.

The Renaissance Man

Leonardo was also a sculptor, musician, architect, and engineer. He accompanied princes on their voyages and into battles. He also designed plans for things that were so difficult to understand that nobody could make them – a clumsy car, a small submarine and a rickety aeroplane!

Often Leonardo did not finish his projects. If he had finished the statue he drew up for the Duke of Milan, he would have made a rearing horse as big as a house.

Sketch of a bombard

Leonardo outpainting Verrocchio.

Statue of the Duke of Milan.

Perspective

A balanced picture: the people are divided equally.

Looking at Roman paintings helped Renaissance artists to rediscover perspective. Perspective creates an illusion of depth in a picture.

Now artists had a set of rules that worked out mathematically how

After **Raphael**, Italian (1483-1520): *The School of Athens*. (Vatican, Rome)

32

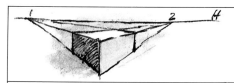

much larger the figures in the fore-ground of a picture should be.

Aristotle and Plato are shown by the portraits of Michelangelo and Leonardo at the apex of the con-struction lines in Raphael's famous fresco.

An unbalanced pic-ture: Raphael would never have constructed his pic-ture like this.

Michelangelo
Italian (1475-1564)

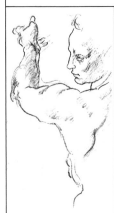

After a study of **Michelangelo** for the ceiling of the Sistine Chapel.

Michelangelo and Pope Julius II.

Michelangelo was a famous Florentine sculptor and like Leonardo da Vinci he was also an engineer, a poet and, of course, a painter.

Michelangelo was ordered by Pope Julius II to decorate the ceiling of the Sistine Chapel in his Vatican palace in Rome. Michelangelo, having at first accepted the work reluctantly, decided to astonish the world.

Perched on scaffolding 20 metres above the floor, virtually alone, he painted over 300 colossal figures filling an area the size of a football pitch in four years. An extraordinary achievement, especially since he had to work with his head cricked back all the time. A position he became so used to that when he received a letter at that time, he had to hold it over his head and bend backwards to read it.

On the end wall is his Last Judgement – Jesus Christ in the middle judging which people should go to heaven and which to hell. Usually this subject was painted near the exit to a church, to remind you of what could happen should you not return. Michelangelo painted it above the altar.

Colour

Describe a colour. It's difficult, isn't it? We can say it is blue like the sky or red like a poppy, but there are hundreds of different blues and reds, so we give names to them. Sky blue, navy blue, royal blue, powder blue, cornflower blue. What is the colour of the lady's sleeve in Van Eyck's picture on page 20? We could call it 'Van Eyck blue' couldn't we? (There is a Veronese green, named after a famous Italian painter.)

Classification of colours

Colours are divided into two categories: primary and secondary. There are three primary colours (1). They are **red, blue and yellow.** You cannot get these by mixing two other colours together. To get purple, green and orange, you have to mix primary colours together, which give us secondary colours (2). Blues and greens are cold colours, red and yellow are warm colours.

Mixing colours

Get out your paint box – mix together two primary colours. Now add black. The colour becomes less intense, less clear. Now mix together the same two colours and add white. The colour becomes chalkier.

If we paint red next to green and red next to brown, the first makes the red look stronger, the second makes

1   2

1 + black   2 + black
1 + white   2 + white

Look at how colours affect each other when placed side by side. The skill is knowing which colours to put next to which to create the desired effect.

the red look weaker, so if a painter wants something to stand out, he will not paint a red coat next to a brown wall for instance. Also, if you put a warm colour square like red, on top of a cold coloured square like blue, the red will look as if it is in front of the blue, which is why in Dutch paintings very often red houses are painted against a cool background to give the painting some life.

List of paints that Vincent Van Gogh asked his brother Theo to buy for him:
20 large tubes of flake white
10 large tubes of zinc white
15 double tubes of malachite green
10 Chrome yellow, lemon
10 Chrome yellow (No.2)
3 Vermilion
6 little tubes of geranium lake } *newly*
12 crimson lake *pounded*
2 carmine
4 little tubes of Prussian blue
4 little tubes of Cinnabar green
   (very light)

Red and green: the red is more alive

Red and yellow: the red is less alive

A red square (warm colour) inside a green square (cold colour): the red jumps forward.

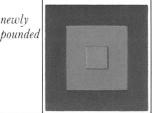

Venice

Venice, in northern Italy, has no roads; it is criss-crossed with canals, lined by lavishly coloured palaces. It is a city of light and reflected light, as the colours shimmer and blend into each other.

When the Renaissance came to Venice, then a wealthy trading port, Venetian painters concentrated on light and colour rather than the planning, drawing and reality of Florence or Rome. Is this surprising?

The water makes everything damp, so frescoes would crumble away. The forests are a long way away, so nearly all the great paintings were done, not on wood panels, but on **canvas**, a cloth which is stretched over a frame and coated with *size* – a type of white glue – before being painted. Some of the great Venetian painters were the **Bellini** brothers (c. 1430-c. 1516), **Giorgione** (1477-1510) and **Titian** (1487-1576). Here is the great Giorgione in his studio overlooking a canal, painting the *Concert champêtre*, which now hangs in the Louvre.

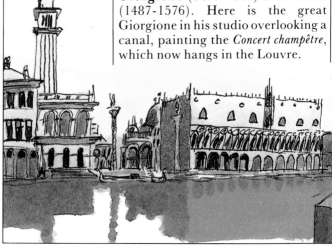

38

After **Giorgione**, Italian (1477-1510): *Concert champêtre*. Giorgione's short career is very mysterious. Only about 5 or 6 pictures definitely by him have survived. By painting small canvasses of figures in a landscape he introduced a new dimension into painting.

Titian
Italian (1487-1576)

Paintings of nude girls (here it is *Danae*) were often covered by curtains so as not to offend the ladies.

Titian learnt to paint in Giorgione's studio. Unlike his master he lived to the age of 86. In this time he produced hundreds of paintings and drawings.

Titian's style was very free and easy. Often he had only a rough idea of what he would paint before he started. And unlike the Florentines, he rarely drew out a design. This was partly because the oil paint used in Venice could be painted over for corrections and changes, whereas tempera used in Florence could not, so they had to plan their pictures very carefully beforehand. Titian sometimes even finished off paintings with his fingers, hurling his brushes aside in his enthusiasm.

Titian was most famous for his use of colour and his portraits. Here these qualities are combined in his famous *Charles V on horseback*. The great Emperor was so struck by Titian's genius that they became friends much to everyone's envy and jealousy. 'Who does this Titian think he is?' they said. And: 'Do you know, when Titian dropped his brush, His Most Holy and Majesterial Excellency actually bent down and picked it up!'

Far left: *Charles V on horseback* (Prado, Madrid) ● Painted after Charles V had won a great battle, it is not just a likeness of Charles, but a portrait glorifying him.

The master and his followers from all centuries.

41

Mannerism

Oops, you think that I'm going to fall off the page don't you? Well I can't really because it's only an illusion. An invention of the artist. Why should an artist want to create these illusions?

With Leonardo, Michelangelo and Raphael the Renaissance lasted 100 years and it was 100 years of perfection. Could anyone do better? Three Roman painters, Parmigiano, Pontormo and Bronzino decided that there was only one way to go. They started by copying the grand masters of the Renaissance while exaggerating their style. Mannerism was born.

These painters made all the bodies look twisted, elongated and bulky. The laws of perspective no longer applied, figures in the foreground were sometimes tiny, those in the background huge against smaller bits of architecture. The colours tended to be busy and harsh.

Illusion is an important element in Mannerist painting. The stamp on the left looks normal doesn't it? If you turn the book upside down you can see where Mannerism has come to rest. Mannerism really only lasted from 1520 to 1600. It was confined mainly to Rome and was followed by the Baroque style.

After **Mitelli:**
Reversible portrait.

Parmigianino, Italian (1503-1540).
Pontormo, Italian (1494-1557).
Bronzino, Italian (1503-1572).

The figures in this impression of Mannerism by the illustrator twist into impossible angles while naked athletes try to escape from the illusion. A line of useless columns of uncertain size support emptiness. *Putti* play under the watchful gaze of a relaxing faun.

Caravaggio
Italian (1573-1610)

Right: *The Death of the Virgin Mary* ●
(Louvre, Paris)

Poor Caravaggio, what a life! He lost a tennis match and stabbed his opponent. So he fled to Malta via Naples. In Malta, his paintings were very well received, but he ruined everything by assaulting a judge. He escaped from prison and, returning to Naples, he was stabbed in a fight. Left for dead, he recovered and sailed to Port' Ercole. Here he was imprisoned – by mistake. When he was released, he saw a boat sailing away with all that he owned – or so he thought. He was so angry he had a seizure and a few days later he died, aged 37. His belongings had been waiting for him at customs all the time.

Meanwhile, Caravaggio was a wonderful painter. He wanted to paint things as they were.

In this painting, Jesus Christ's sad disciples are simple peasants mourning the dead Virgin Mary. People say that Caravaggio used the body of a prostitute drowned in the Tiber in Rome as a model for the dead Virgin. You can imagine the outcry! But Caravaggio insisted that, after all, the disciples *were* peasants and the Virgin *was* dead. Whilst the Church argued, other painters copied Caravaggio's style.

The *Baroque* style (c. 1600-1750) unites architecture, painting and sculpture. Its scrolls and curves, the use of light and dark (*chiaroscuro*), involve the spectator in an emotional experience.

Still Life

There had been still lifes in the Ancient World in the form of mosaics, but the tradition died out until it returned to Holland in the 17th century. Our title 'still life' derives from the Dutch *still-leven*.

There are many types of still life, but by and large it was not popular in southern Europe. It was considered the lowest form of art in France (hence it is called 'dead nature') and in England was not popular until the second half of the 19th century by which time it was thought that 'a well painted turnip was better than a badly painted Madonna'.

However, in the 1890s still lifes came into their own again, first with the Impressionists who highlighted the sensual appeal of the sparkling textures of fruit and vegetables and the Cubists who used the domesticity of a still life as a familiar reference point for the spectator faced with such an unfamiliar view.

After a still life by **Cézanne** (1), and **Picasso** (2).

After **Rembrandt,** Dutch (1606-1669): *Portrait of Titus*.

Painting of everyday life in the tavern, home or at school is known as 'genre' painting. Often the picture will contain a message. For instance the message from the picture on the right, painted in 1567, of the peasant, scholar and soldier is that if you are lazy and greedy, you will not achieve much in life. At the same time it is a scene which depicts everyday life.

Scenes from my life

After **Brueghel,** Flemish (1525-1569): *Land of Cockaigne.*

Like still life painting, genre painting started in Holland.

Here on the left you can see a school scene. Rembrandt's son Titus, aged 13, is sitting at a desk holding a leather inkwell. Titus hated being a model for his father. Eventually they made a bargain. If Titus sat as a model for Rembrandt, he wouldn't have to do the shopping that week.

Portraits

Rembrandt, *The Anatomy Lesson* •

After **van Eyck,** *The Betrothal of the Arnolfini.*

Portraits are pictures of real people. They always show the face and often the hands because these are the most expressive parts of the body.

Before there were cameras, patrons commissioned portraits of their children, wives, lovers or of themselves. But portraits did not really become a fashion until houses were big enough to hold them. By the 17th century, though, portrait painting had become highly popular. Portraits helped show off the superiority of the family. In great houses, portraits were hung in passageways or on the walls of the main staircases where visitors would see them and admire the wealth and importance of the family's ancestors. These portraits were less to evoke a likeness than to assert rank.

In 17th century Holland, group

One of the greatest miniature painters was a handsome Englishman called Nicholas Hilliard (1547-1619). He has left us pictures of Sir Walter Raleigh, Queen Elizabeth I and Sir Francis Drake amongst others. They can be seen in the National Portrait Gallery, London.

portraits were the fashion. The officers of the wealthy guilds had their portraits painted in a group and shared the expense. Perhaps the greatest master of this type of portrait was Rembrandt. This picture is *The Anatomy Lesson* (1631). *Dr. Tulp* shows the arm muscles of a dead man to his colleagues in the hospital. Which is the only man in the picture watching the dissection? Notice the use of contrasting dark and light, known as *chiaroscuro*. It can also be seen in the picture by Caravaggio (see page 44).

Finally there were the painted equivalents of the photographs of loved ones kept in the wallet. Tiny miniature portraits were painted to fit into a little medallion.

After an 18th century portrait.

After **Modigliani,** French (1884-1920).

Self-portraits

Rembrandt copying his reflection from a mirror.

After **Velasquez**, Spanish (1599-1660): *Las Meninas*.

Self-portraits are fascinating because they show us the painters themselves. The first picture here is one of over 70 self-portraits by Rembrandt. You can see he has pulled a face (1). He made a series of pictures at this time showing himself with different expressions to practise his technique, using himself as a model!

Gustave Courbet (1819-1877) appears a serious young man (2). He wanted people to take his new style of 'Realism' seriously.

Rubens (1577-1640) shows himself with his beautiful wife Isabella in rich clothes (3). This is so that when people see this picture they will remember he was a gentleman. This is very different from the Van Gogh portrait (4). Why is his ear bandaged?

Vincent Van Gogh was a lonely person. One night he had a terrible argument with his friend, the painter Paul Gauguin. In a frenzy of misery, he cut off a bit of his left ear.

Throughout his life, Rembrandt painted himself over 70 times. Gradually we can see him change from a talented, self-confident youth to a thoughtful, sad old man.

He painted this self-portrait afterwards. Artists paint themselves from their reflection in the mirror. Vincent's right ear appears to be bandaged, because when he was painting his reflection the image was reversed.

The last portrait, by Rembrandt (5), is very different from the first.

Finally Velasquez (left) has painted himself while painting. His picture *Las Meninas* is both a group portrait (the Infanta of Spain surrounded by her ladies-in-waiting) and a self-portrait.

1. Rembrandt ●
2. Courbet ●
3. Rubens ●
4. Van Gogh ●
5. Rembrandt ●
6. Anonymous!

Landscape

After a landscape by **Claude Lorrain,** French (1600–1682), left, and by **A. Cozens**, English (1717–86), right.

Alexander Cozens, an English painter, splattered ink on a piece of paper and then made up landscapes from the shapes it suggested.

The ideal landscape

There have always been landscapes in paintings, but until the 17th century they were only there as a setting for the people. Gradually, though, the background moved further and further into the foreground. It was in 17th and 18th century Holland that landscapes, just like still lifes, first came to be painted entirely without people in them. In France the great landscape painter Claude Lorrain used landscape to help tell his stories – in this case (below) the expulsion of Hagar.

Natural landscapes

Two hundred years separate Claude Lorrain (left) from Courbet (below). Bit by bit artists like Courbet had started to paint landscapes as they really appeared. Courbet believed in painting only what was around him, but the public were not ready for this 'revolutionary' concept and were very unpleasant about his landscapes. People said the cliffs in his landscape (below) looked like slabs of cheese. The public was even more unpleasant about the way his Impressionist successors, like Monet and Cézanne, treated nature.

Courbet, French (1819-1877): *The Cliffs at Etretat After a Storm* ●
(Louvre, Paris)

The Le Nain brothers

Here are the three Le Nain brothers: Antoine, Louis and Mathieu: the inseparable brothers (but look, my friends, I have the key!). All three work in the same studio and the pictures are all signed 'Le Nain' making it very difficult to decide which brother painted which picture. They specialized in pictures of 17th century peasants: peasants in their houses and in the fields. Their pictures are full of life and warmth. You can see here how the peasants are rushing to admire the Le Nains' latest work.

The **Le Nain** brothers 'photo-graphing' a family of peasants.

Painters of Realism

They lived at the same time as Claude Lorrain and were unusual

Their peers also thought highly of the Le Nain brothers: all three of them were elected members of the Academy on its foundation in 1648. The shock must have been too great for Antoine and Louis. They died later that year.

for the time in that they painted things very realistically, like a photograph. Yet their paintings were immensely popular, at least from 1620 to 1660 and then suddenly they fell from favour and were forgotten until the 1770s when peasant scenes were again in demand.

Antoine, Louis and Mathieu **Le Nain,** French (17th century).

William Hogarth

English (1697-1764)

A

B

C

Hogarth

William Hogarth was the first great English-born painter and was especially popular on account of his moral and satirical paintings. What do you think those lines on the left are? It's a man with a spear over his shoulder (B), walking through a door (A) with his dog (C). Many painters of the time painted outside but Hogarth worked mostly in his studio from sketches made outside. Instead of sketching in detail, he developed a visual shorthand using single lines so that when he got back to his studio he could remember the positions of people. Then he would make a proper painting of, in this case, a soldier and his dog entering a room.

Hogarth the satirist

Hogarth is most famous for his sequence of paintings that tell a story. Stories, even fairy stories, often have morals to them, telling us how to behave. The polite princess gets the prince. Hogarth painted stories about the life of the time, which warned people not to go off with lots of women, or spend too much money, or eat and drink too much. They were very popular because they were so funny. Each one is like a stage with actors in a play.

I am looking at a series of pictures called *Marriage à la Mode*. It is as well to be enthusiastic about them because Mr. Hogarth is incredibly bad-tempered (and so is his dog . . . ugh!). Once a man made Hogarth so furious that Hogarth bit him.

The elegance of the Eighteenth Century

1. **David,** French, (1748–1825): *The Coronation of Napoleon* ●

2. **Watteau,** French (1684–1721): *Gilles* ●

showing the wistfulness of Rococo to perfection.

3. **Fragonard,** French (1732–1806): the charm of Rococo lives in *The Swing* ● (Petit-Palais, Paris).

The huge palace of Versailles near Paris in France was created for one of the greatest French kings, Louis XIV. He had the palace built along the purest classical lines. On Louis' death this grand style died with him. Painters longed to paint lighter, more flexible pictures, in clear colours. Freshness, sublety and frivolity were the order of the day.

Perfect examples of this new style, **Rococo,** are Boucher's (1703–1770) delicious portrait of Madame de Pompadour and Fragonard's intimate country scenes. It was also at this time that Monsieur Watteau painted me.

Frivolity doesn't last long, the same was true of Rococo. No sooner had it started (1715) than it stopped (1740).

It was replaced by the seriousness of **Neoclassicism** as propounded by the great French painter Jacques-Louis David. In 1748 the ruins of the Roman towns of Pompeii and Herculaneum were discovered. Everyone wanted classical pictures. But unlike Renaissance painters who worked from engravings of classical art, the 'new classicists' copied freshly excavated examples of Greek and Roman statues and architecture.

The photographs of paintings in this book are not that size
in real life! To help you see the scale of them, I am
standing by these three. For example, David's *Coronation* is
so huge that Napoleon is pictured larger than life-size.

1

2

3 —

Light and shade

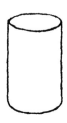

After **David**,
French
(1748-1825),
*Napoleon Crossing
the Alps*.

David lived a long time and must have been very clever to have survived at the height of his craft for so long: in the beginning he was for the king, who was guillotined in the revolution. David then supported the revolution. Next he became a favourite of Napoleon. Mainly because he always painted him to look like a Roman emperor.

Here we see Napoleon posing on a model horse (a real one never stands still) for David's picture *Napoleon crossing the Alps*. David is trying to finish the picture as quickly as possible because Napoleon is getting impatient, and he knows only too well the ferocious rages of the emperor.

David became the most influential painter in Europe. He only had to paint a picture of a woman wearing a particular style of dress and within days the whole of Paris was wearing it.

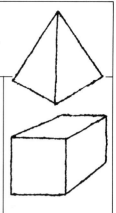

In this painting David uses the same *chiaroscuro* effect as Rembrandt and Caravaggio. This has the effect of making the object look rounder.

If you take a pencil and shade one side of the cube or pyramid, they will look much more solid, and if then you shade the paper as if the cube, pyramid and tube were casting a shadow, they will look even more real.

63

Academy of Art

David, French (1748–1825).

Ingres, French (1780–1867).

After **David**
1. *Monsieur de Sériziat*
2. *Mme de Récamier*

After **Ingres**
3. *Mlle Rivière*
4. *La Source*

Napoleon liked the paintings of David and his pupil Dominique Ingres (1780–1867), because they flattered him and his court. He encouraged the rich men and women of the time to buy them, and to hang them in special public rooms.

The new Academies

As a result David and Ingres became very rich and powerful. David started new Academies to pass on new 'rules' of painting as he saw them. But he banned younger painters who did not follow his 'rules', and so ruined their careers.

Talented rebels

But fortunately, as so often in art, there was a faction of young talent prepared to rebel against these strict 'rules'. And finally in 1815, when Napoleon fell, David and Ingres fled the country. (Ingres later returned, David died in 1825 in Brussels.) The **Romantics** as they called themselves took their chance.

Romantic painters wanted a freer approach to art. They wanted to paint with the imagination – they wanted the exact opposite of the neoclassicists – feelings and emotions, heroes and drama, excitement and energy.

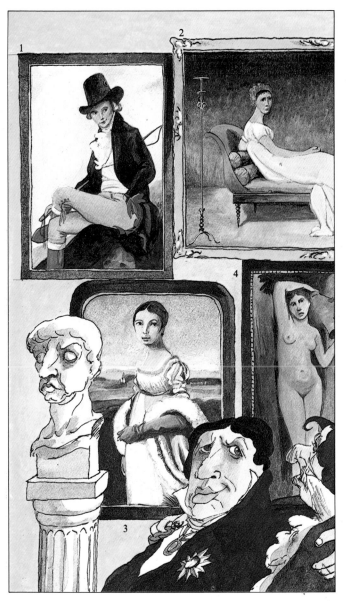

The Raft of the 'Medusa'

Theodore Géricault was one of the most impressive Romantic artists. He painted the enormous *Raft of the 'Medusa'* in 1819.

What angle and what moment of a given theme a painter has chosen to paint is very important. It tells you what the painter himself finds interesting. Tony Ross, in the picture opposite, has chosen to illustrate a different moment in the story from the one Géricault depicted in his famous painting (overleaf). Read the account of what happened. Which moment would you have chosen to show?

The story of the *Medusa*

On 2 July 1816, the French ship *Medusa* set off for Senegal in Africa. But the boat ran aground off West Africa. There were not enough lifeboats, so 149 men and one woman were forced to board a makeshift raft, which should have been pulled by the two lifeboats. But the crew of the lifeboats rowed away. All they had on board the raft were some casks of wine. For ten days they floated without any food, terrified and drunk. Then they spotted a ship – the *Argus*. Frantically they waved, but the ship never saw them. Eventually 5 days later, the *Argus* found the fifteen survivors.

Géricault, French (1791–1824).

He died at the age of 33 after falling off his horse.

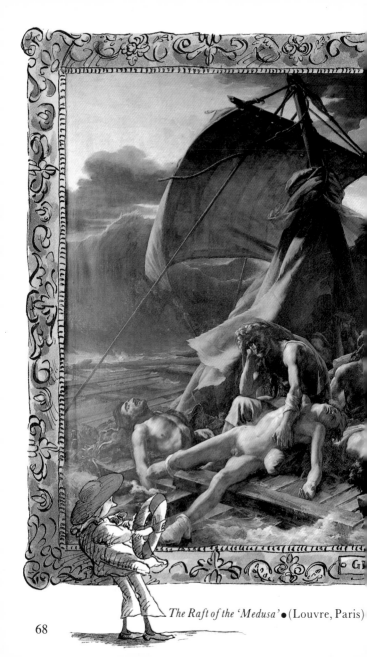

The Raft of the 'Medusa' •(Louvre, Paris)

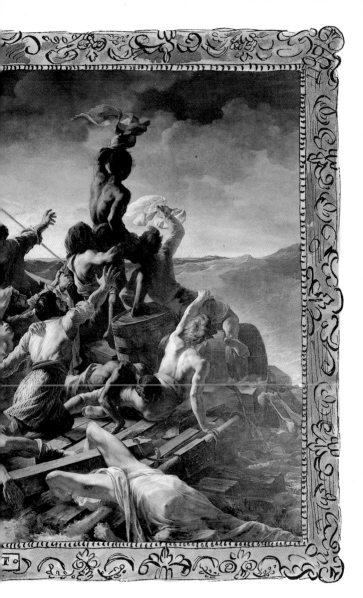

The picture is immense: it measures 7.16m by 4.91m.

I wanted to show what such a scene was like. I got the sailors to lash me to the mast to observe it; I was lashed for 4 hours and I did not expect to escape; but I felt bound to record it if I did.

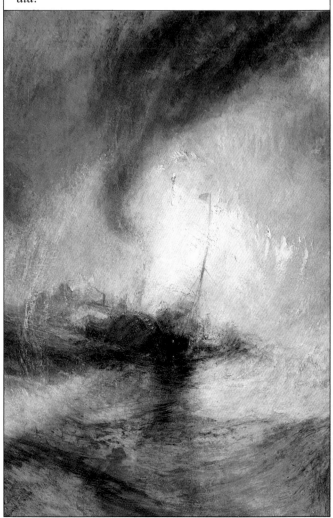

J.M.W. Turner

English (1775–1851)

This is how J.M.W. Turner, the great English Romantic painter, described how he came to paint this stormy scene. Obviously, tied to the mast, he was not able to sketch anything. But in this seascape, he is painting *what it was like* to be there. An impression. This was a new approach to landscape painting. As Turner got older his paintings became even wilder, more impressionistic and exceedingly beautiful, especially his watercolours.

Unfortunately, very few other people liked this way of painting. This picture, for instance, was condemned as 'soapsuds and whitewash'.

Turner died a recluse under an assumed name in a London boarding house.

Today, however, he is recognized for the innovator he was. His complete works are housed in the Turner Collection in Somerset House. A fitting monument to one of England's greatest painters.

Turner making a sketch of his father (who was a barber).

Left: *Snowstorm at Sea* ● (National Gallery, London)

War reporters

Seen here on the hill (1) Gros, (2) Goya, (3) Delacroix (4) Géricault,

War in the early 19th century was not the same as it is today. Individual soldiers could distinguish themselves in combat. Each army took along painters to depict the scene. They would sit in the hills above and watch the action.

Here you see Baron Gros, official painter to Napoleon, immortalizing his emperor in one of his campaigns.

Delacroix summed up the position of the Romantics in relation to the Neoclassicism of David when he said: 'I am a rebel not a revolutionary'.

Next to him, Francisco Goya, the Spanish painter, is completing a much more horrible and sombre picture called *The Firing Squad*.

Géricault arrives brandishing his passionate portrait of an officer in the Imperial Guard, while Delacroix works on his *Massacre de Scio*.

Van Gogh wrote of Delacroix: 'Only Rembrandt and Delacroix could paint the face of Christ'.

Gros, French (1771–1835).

Goya, Spanish (1746–1828).

Delacroix, French (1798–1863).

Géricault, French (1791–1824).

Watercolour

The art of watercolour painting was perfected by the English Romantic painters of the early 19th century, particularly Turner and Constable (1776–1837).

A box of watercolours, brushes and paper can easily be fitted into a little light satchel, and so it is a very convenient way of painting out of doors. Many watercolours are small landscape scenes.

The range of effects that can be achieved is very wide. The main difference to oil painting is that to make colours paler you do not add white paint, but dilute them with water, so that you see the white paper behind.

Blocks of watercolour in a box and a tube of watercolour.

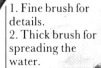

1. Fine brush for details.
2. Thick brush for spreading the water.

'Ah, this is the life, basking by an oasis, but I do miss home' . . .

This scene gives some idea of the range of effects that can be achieved using watercolour – from the soporific luminosity of the desert to the dense deep tones of an English autumn.

The five greatest English watercolourists were **Cozens** (1752–97), **Girtin** (1775–1802), **Constable** (1776–1837), **Cotman** (1782–1842) and **Turner** (1775-1851). All had slightly different techniques but Turner's was the most daring. He used solid colour freely, wiped partially dry colour with rags and scratched the surface of the paper with a knife to get extra lights.

The Impressionists

1. After **Edouard Manet,** French (1832–1883): *A Bar at the Folies-Bergères.*

2. After **Pierre-Auguste Renoir,** French (1841–1919): *Claude Monet reading.*

3. After **Claude Monet,** French (1840–1926): *Impression, Sunrise.*

4. After **Alfred Sisley,** English (1839–1899): *Wheatfields near Argenteuil.*

'Quelle horreur!' And there were many other exclamations, insults, and jeers that greeted the first exhibition of Impressionist painting in 1874. A journalist reviewing the exhibition called them 'Impressionists' as an insult, mocking a picture by Monet titled *Impression, Sunrise.* But bit by bit the public became used to this new type of painting and eventually came to love it.

What exactly was this new type of painting? Impressionism was about light and colour. These

Eugène Delacroix, earlier in the 19th century, had noticed that a red object will have green in its shadow, a blue object – orange and so on. The Impressionists took this principle and exaggerated it.

painters were not interested in the exact physical form of an object, they wanted to create objects using just light and colour. They achieved this by applying the paint in small brightly-coloured dabs with no firm outline even in the shadows.

All the Impressionists wanted was to 'make of their art something solid and durable, like the art of the museums'. They certainly succeeded.

5. After **Camille Pissarro,** French (1830–1903): *Lordship Lane Station.*

Cézanne
French (1839–1906)

'With an apple I will shock Paris!' said Cézanne. Cézanne liked painting apples in his still lifes. Like the Dutch painters, he was aware of the power of familiar objects. Over and over again he represented the same things: apples, oranges, onions in a jug of flowers . . . He worked relentlessly with incredible single-mindedness.

Out of this developed a style which made his famous apples, shown from a number of angles at once, appear to be sliding off the table – 'crooked fruit in drunken pots'. It was not surprising that the public were astonished, this was a completely new way of representing objects. He was the creator of modern 20th century painting.

Cézanne
Self-portrait ●

After a still life by Cézanne.

Van Gogh
Dutch (1853–1890)

Vincent Van Gogh came from Holland. At first he painted very dark pictures. But when he went to France, everything changed. He painted landscapes and portraits in very bright colours. Then he met the French painter Paul Gauguin, who influenced him to paint things with less definite shapes and in harsher colours.

Van Gogh, *Self-portrait with Ear Cut Off* ●

Van Gogh lived alone. But, so as to share his feelings about painting and his work with the people he loved, he wrote hundreds of letters. (See his letter to his brother Theo p.37). He wrote to Paul Gauguin about the picture on the right:

A cypress tree with a star . . ., a lustrous moon in a night sky, a thin crescent moon barely piercing the thick shadow cast by the earth – a star of pronounced brightness, with soft greens and pinks in an ultramarine sky covered by scudding clouds. At the bottom, the road is hedged by tall yellow reeds, behind the low blue Alps stretch towards an old inn with orange-lit windows and above all a very high cypress tree, very straight, very dark.

Vincent van Gogh shot himself a few weeks after painting this picture.

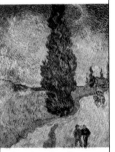

Road with a Cypress tree ●

Picasso
Spanish (1881–1973)

Right: *Maya with her doll*●
(Picasso Museum, Paris)

Glass of wine.

'Cubist' glass of wine.

Pablo Picasso was born in Spain in 1881, but lived most of his life in France.

No painter since the Renaissance and the discovery of perspective has more radically transformed the nature of painting. He stands with Cézanne at the beginning of a new age.

Picasso had discovered a new way of representing an object in three dimensions on a picture surface. This revolution is called **'Cubism'**, a name given to the movement by the critics to mock the pictures that at the time they couldn't understand.

When Picasso painted a glass, a house or a guitar they looked like cubes because he painted these objects from all angles at the 'same' time.

Picasso lived for a long time and throughout his life he experimented in many artistic fields. But though he transformed the styles of 20th century painting as he passed through them he was not interested in staying with a 'style', as such. He had to keep moving on: 'To hell with style,' he used to say. 'Has God got a style?'

This picture of his daughter Maya with her doll was painted by Picasso in 1938. You can see one of the characteristics of Picasso's Cubist painting, two eyes – one viewed from the side, one from the front.

To me there is no past or future in art ... The art of the Greeks, of the Egyptians, of the great painters who lived in other times is more alive today than it ever was.

Picasso, 1923.

In the picture, the painting on the left is one of Picasso's earliest ones. The one on the right was painted at the age of 80, 50 years after Picasso had discovered Cubism.

Three favourite subjects of Picasso were the clown, harlequin and monk. Can you spot the great man in the picture?

Magritte
Belgian (1898-1967)

For many children (and a few grown-ups) a mountain could have the form of an eagle. For Magritte too . . .

A little grain of madness

Magritte's images all have a grain of madness and of freedom. Anything can be turned into anything and why not: women into fish, birds into leaves. Even rocks take the liberty of floating on water.

'Everybody has their little ideas' said Magritte. And it is these little ideas of Magritte that shock us, make us laugh and make life more fun.

After
The Son of Man

Magritte has written *This is not a pipe*, which is quite true. It is a *painting* of a pipe.

▼

Ceci n'est pas une pipe.

Pop art

Pop art started in New York at the beginning of the sixties. What did it show? Advertisements, magazines, comics, cinema, rock 'n' roll, urban life and so on. Like Magritte and his famous pipe, the American pop artists showed objects of the utmost banality, each one a mirror of the industrial society that produced it. The mirror never lies.

After **Andy Warhol**
1. *Dick Tracy*
2. *Elvis*
3. *Campbell's soup can.*

After **Roy Lichtenstein**
4. *Sweet dreams, baby!*

Signing off

From the time of the Renaissance, instead of staying anonymous like the artists of the Middle Ages, painters signed their pictures. Often they made up crafty signatures out of their initials or names. The painter Bernardo Daddi (in Italian, 'dice') signs himself with a dice (1). Albrecht Dürer signs with his initials and the date (2).

But before you see a signature, you can recognise a painter just from his style. The pictures by Mondrian (1872–1944) are often a pattern of primary colours (3). Most of Toulouse-Lautrec's pictures bear the witty style of the caricature (4). You can see another example, adapted by Tony Ross, on the cover.

3

1

1525

2

A mini-guide to museum visiting

As long ago as 500 BC in the city of Athens there were collections of the masterpieces of great artists open to the public. Because in Greece the goddesses of the Arts were called Muses, the 'Temple of the Muses' was the place where the collections of these beautiful objects were kept, hence 'Museum'.

But the buildings that we think of today as Museums were not seen in Europe until the 19th century.

After the French Revolution in 1793 a decree announced the opening up to the public of the Louvre Palace which contained the fabulous royal collection. The Louvre was born, the first of the modern museums.

Famous European Museums

Paris
Louvre
Musée d'Art moderne
Jeu de Paume
Centre Pompidou
Madrid
Prado
Florence
Uffizzi
Venice
Academia
Munich
Alte Pinakothek

Which museum should you visit?

A museum does not have to be famous to be interesting. Before you set out in search of the large museums of London and Europe first visit your local museum and explore its treasures.

How should you visit them?

Paintings are like books, music, or even food: your tastes change, your enthusiasms and moods come and go. One day you feel like soaking yourself in huge battle scenes, the next puzzling over abstract paintings. It is best to follow your whim, otherwise you

86

Some British Museums National Gallery, London. The Tate Gallery, London. National Portrait Gallery, London. Ashmolean Museum, Oxford. Fitzwilliam Museum, Cambridge. Walker Art Gallery, Liverpool. Scottish National Gallery, Edinburgh. Alnwick Castle, Alnwick. City Museum, Birmingham.

won't really see what you are looking at. It is also better to see a few pictures because you are interested in them than dozens just because they're there. It is a good idea to return to look at the pictures you already know and like. Each time you will view them differently and discover new details you've never seen before. Also the pictures that you have difficulty understanding today will reveal their secrets bit by bit.

Brussels
Musées royaux des Beaux Arts

Amsterdam
Rijksmuseum

A panorama of painters in history

15,000 BC Cave
paintings at Lascaux.

4000 BC First writing.

2600 BC Pyramid of
Cheops built in Egypt.

AD 43 Britain invaded
by Romans.

570 Muhammad,
founder of Islam, born
in Mecca.

878 King Alfred
defeats the Danes.

1066 Battle of
Hastings. William the
Conqueror becomes
King of England.

1300 Frescoes of
Giotto.

1450 Birth of
Hieronymus Bosch.

1453 Hundred Years'
War ends. Siege of
Constantinople. End of
the Middle Ages.

1450 Johann
Gutenberg invents
movable-type printing.

1471 Birth of Albrecht
Dürer.

1492 Christopher
Columbus discovers
America.

1507 Leonardo paints
the *Mona Lisa*.

1509 Raphael paints
The School of Athens.

1512 Michelangelo finishes decorating the Sistine chapel.

1564 Birth of William Shakespeare.

1576 Death of Titian.

1588 Spanish Armada defeated by the English.

1649 Execution of Charles I of England.

1669 Death of Rembrandt.

1717 Watteau paints *Gilles*.

1718 Bach writes *1st Brandenburg Concerto*.

1726 Swift writes *Gulliver's Travels*.

1756 Birth of Mozart.

1765 James Watt's steam engine.

1775 American War of Independence.

1789 French Revolution.

1804 Beethoven composes his *Heroic Symphony*.

1805 David paints *The Coronation of Napoleon*.

1815 Battle of Waterloo.

1839 Daguerre invents photography.

1872 Monet paints *Impression, Sunrise*.

1891 Sir Arthur Conan Doyle writes *The Adventures of Sherlock Holmes*.

1903 Orville and Wilbur Wright make the first flight in an aeroplane.

1907 Picasso paints his first 'Cubist' painting *Les Demoiselles d'Avignon*.

Index

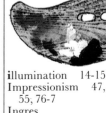

The author and the illustrator

After finishing a degree in the History of Art and Philosophy at London University, **Adrian Sington** worked in a children's bookshop in London before going into publishing. He has written and edited many books for children and adults on history, ancient civilizations and the history of art and architecture. He is married with two children and lives in London. In the summer he indulges his passion for cricket.

Tony Ross has been one of the leading children's book illustrators in England since the publication of his first picture-book in 1973. A great number of his 50-plus picture-books have been published in many different countries. *Painting and Painters*, though, is his first information book. He comes to it with a wealth of experience in teaching art, having been for many years Senior Lecturer in Art at Manchester, where he has taught many young artists who have become illustrators in their own right today. He lives in Devon with his wife and daughter.

Acknowledgements

The editor and publishers wish to thank the Museums, Galleries, Private Collections and Agencies for permission to reproduce the following paintings and photographs to which they hold the copyright:

20. *The Betrothal of the Arnolfini*, Jan Van Eyck (National Gallery, London). 22–3. *The Haywain*, Hieronymus Bosh (Prado Museum, Madrid). 30–31. *Mona Lisa*, Leonardo daVinci (Musées Nationaux, Paris). *The Proportions of Man. Sketch of a bombard*, Leonardo da Vinci (Photo Mazzo). 40. *Charles V on Horseback*, Titian (Prado Museum, Madrid). 44. *Death of the Virgin*, Caravaggio (Musées Nationaux, Paris). 50. *The Anatomy Lesson*, Rembrandt (Mauritshuis Museum, The Hague). 53. *Self Portrait*, Rembrandt (British Museum, London). *Man with a leather belt*, Courbet (Musées Nationaux, Paris). *Self-portrait with Isabella Brandt*, Rubens (Photo Giraudon). *Self-portrait with ear cut off*, Van Gogh (Courtauld Collection). *Artist with easel*, Rembrandt (Musées Nationaux, Paris). 55. *Cliffs at Etretat after a storm*, Courbet (Musées Nationaux, Paris). 61. *The Coronation of Napoleon*, David (Musées Nationaux, Paris). *Gilles*, Watteau (Musées Nationaux, Paris). *The Swing*, Fragonard (Photo Giraudon). 68–9. *The Raft of the 'Medusa'*, Géricault (Musées Nationaux, Paris). 70. *Snowstorm at sea*, Turner (National Gallery, London). 78. *Self-portrait*, Cézanna (Photo Giraudon). 79. *Self-portrait with ear cut off*, Van Gogh (Rüksmuseum, Otterlo). 81. *Maya with doll*, Picasso (Photo Emedia, Paris). 82. *Picasso* (Photo André Villers).

Every effort has been made to trace copyright but if any ommissions have been made please let us know in order that we may put it right in the next edition.